D0699401

NO KNOWN SURVIVORS

NO KNOWN

DAVID LEVINE'S

Introduced and Selected by

SURVIVORS

POLITICAL PLANK

JOHN KENNETH GALBRAITH

Gambit
INCORPORATED
Boston
1970

Library of Congress Catalog Card Number: 77-118213

Printed in the United States of America

FIRST PRINTING

What is David Levine's secret? Some people claim that his genius was in getting published regularly by *The New York Review of Books.* The idea being that, if you're next to that prose, or some of it anyway, you can't lose. John Updike offered a somewhat similar theory in his introduction to *Pens and Needles;* he thought that Levine as an artist owed a lot simply to being a painstaking workman in an increasingly sloppy world. There is truth here, but there are other reasons. Like all great caricaturists, Levine has an eye for whatever is even slightly wrong. Then he makes it really wrong. General de Gaulle's nose, by general estimate, is only four or five centimeters more than is reasonable; Levine lets it run across the entire page (page 144). Then he brings Johnson's up to the de Gaulle standard. The Gandhi ears get a similar plug, as does the Everett McKinley Dirksen bouffant (page 108). In real life, Hubert Humphrey has the beginning of a double chin; Levine matures, thickens, and triples it (page 32), and Hubert might just as well stop trying to keep his weight down, for it is Levine's caricature by which he will be remembered.

I also attribute a very great deal to Levine's use of props and artifacts. They are his special grace. Sometimes, as in the case of Churchill's and Castro's cigars, they are merely very large, and among other things accord instant recognition. Churchill (page 125) appears as a very small boy, about six, one would say as a guess. With the cigar, he is unmistakable. Without it, he could be almost any nasty youngster.

But the artifacts from which Levine really gets the mileage are more imaginative, sometimes brilliantly so. Henry VIII's royal robes (page 118) and the interesting fashion in which they are tied in front, are works of art and genius. So is Dirksen's nasturtium, or whatever it is, in the picture mentioned above. Two even more famous artifacts are on adjacent pages in this volume (pages 44 and 45), and both improve on drawings of Lyndon Johnson. One uses the map of Viet Nam as an appendix scar; the other uses a fragment of laurel to crown L.B.J.'s nose. It is a sobering thought (for L.B.J. and Ladybird, anyhow) that Levine in these two portraits may have done for Johnson what Gilbert Stuart did for George Washington. Washington was luckier than Johnson. There is a commendable use of artifacts in the picture of Dean Acheson (page 63), in which he appears with a pen that is patently mightier than any sword. Spiro Agnew has also been given some excellent supporting equipment (pages 13 to 18).

More than any other caricaturist, Levine has a fine eye for fraud. Let a statesman parade false affability, false humility, or false sorrow, and Levine will make it into a mask. In the pictures of President Nixon, affability becomes a terrible put-on, as it is, alas, in real life. Levine also reminds us (page 10), as does the President himself from time to time (after Carswell, for instance), that under that gay and boyish smile there still lurks a very mean man.

No Levine drawing needs ever to be explained; the story is all there. I thought once of giving them explanatory captions; I found that in many cases even identification sounded superfluous. When the head of a client state has our Secretary of State in his pocket, Levine leaves no doubt (page 64) that the head of that state has our man in his pocket.

Historians will celebrate Allen Dulles as an amiable man with a special instinct for disaster. It is all in the picture (page 95), with the amiability in the general aspect and the disasters gracefully inscribed on the pipe. Stalin (page 165 and 166) was once billed as an avuncular figure with whom it would not be too hard to get along. The avuncular aspect survives in these drawings along with something very, very grim.

But most of all, Levine is a man of protest—passionate protest. And these drawings, more than anything else, are a social history of protest—especially as the artist felt it. If he likes someone, that is made evident by a scarcity of drawings. (There is only one serious drawing—page 87—of President Kennedy in this portfolio.) If he merely dislikes someone, the drawings are more numerous but the anger is not there. He regards Spiro Agnew, as I do, as an essentially comic character. When Americans are repressed or otherwise made to suffer for their leaders, it will be by someone more ominous than Spiro. Anyone who can be frightened into silence by Agnew didn't have much to say. That is evident here. The drawings do not flatter the Vice-President, but they lack wham. The same can be said of the drawings of Nelson Rockefeller. Rockefeller has been around so long that he is the only man who still takes Rockefeller really seriously. Levine shows him as most people now regard him—as someone who has become rather funny. Nixon by contrast is worth a real attack, and especially when eating grapes. (It *is* hard, incidentally, to remember a symbolically more callous action by a politician against the unfortunate of the land.)

But in this book it is Hubert Humphrey and Lyndon Johnson who get the business, and it is now not hard to imagine Richard Nixon as a full partner. Their crime is their effort to find a moral gloss for the Viet Nam War. This made Levine very mad.

My personal reactions, partly because I am older and more jaded by efforts over the years to make conscionable the unconscionable, are less strong. I have always rather liked Lyndon Johnson, a regard that has not been fully reciprocated. On Viet Nam it was always easier for me to blame the great foreign policy experts whose business it was to advise the President against disaster and who, instead, urged it. But not Levine. His portraits of Johnson, which are here arranged in order of the increasing doubt and sorrow of the subject, and the deepening anger of the artist, are wonderful.

On occasion, Levine misses. He doesn't quite get Robert Kennedy (pages 88 and 89), and to show that no political bias is involved, he doesn't get Ronald Reagan (page 104), either. But the misses are rare, and a poor picture of Bob Kennedy is part of what might be the best one in this book. It shows Bobby and Gene McCarthy riding out against Lyndon Johnson in 1968 (page 21). Gene spears Johnson with a kind of thoughtful indifference. His mind is somewhere else. Kennedy is more intent on his work. The President's reaction is truly magnificent. He is quite unable to perceive the presence of a mortal wound. Here is the history of the Democratic Party in the first half of 1968.

I have a suggestion about this book. It is not one to be leafed through. I did not really enjoy it until I sat down to study the caricatures and arrange them. Then I learned how much they had to tell. This is a book of pictures that is meant to be read.

CONTENTS

I

The Administration:

Faithful Opponents,
Faithless Supporters,
and
Vice-Versa

The Present President

Running . . .

Running Harder . . .

Running too Hard.

Thinks

Thinks Peace and War

Eats Grapes

Crosses Potomac

Arrives with Trunk

Unpacks Trunk

Is Commander in Chief

And Economist in Chief

Cheers for Spiro

From Spiro to Spiro

Spiro and Friends

Good Game

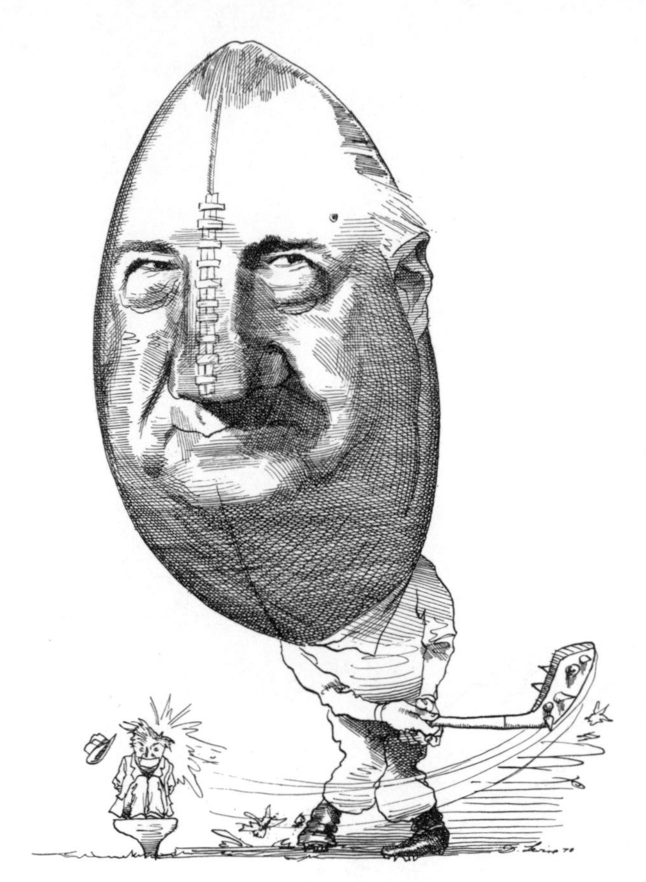

Spiro and Press

McLuhan Delenda Est

Current Friends and Helpers

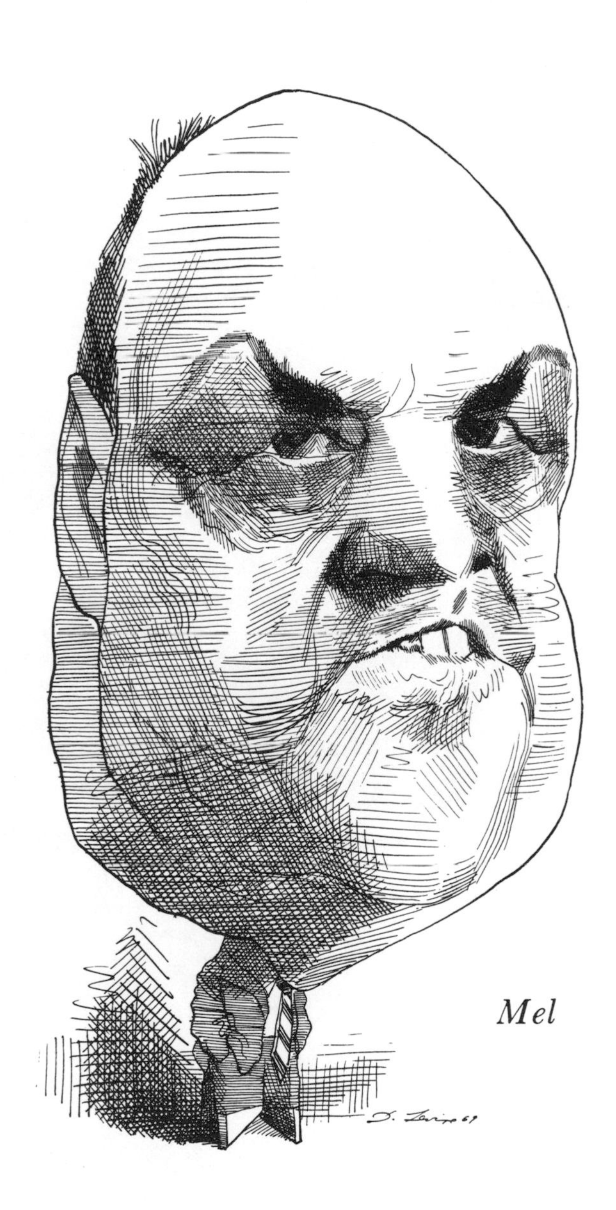

Mel

Mitchell and Silenced Majority

Kissinger and Quick Step

FLASHBACK: CAMPAIGN 1968

Democrats

Republicans

The Ticket

Confrontation in Minneapolis and St. Paul

Center Play

Also Present

CAMPAIGN I:
the Beginning

CAMPAIGN II: *the Middle*

CAMPAIGN III: *the End*

A Small Gallery of Big Losers and Little Winners

Barry

With Toy

With Toys

Rocky: With Props

Without Props

Hubert: Scholar . . .

Statesman . . .

and Strategist.

Policeman Keeps the Peace.

Police Dog . . .

Keeps the Past.

II

Same Play with Original Cast

A Pilgrim's Progress

Bonnie and Clyde

Benevolent Incapacitator

Benevolent Instructor

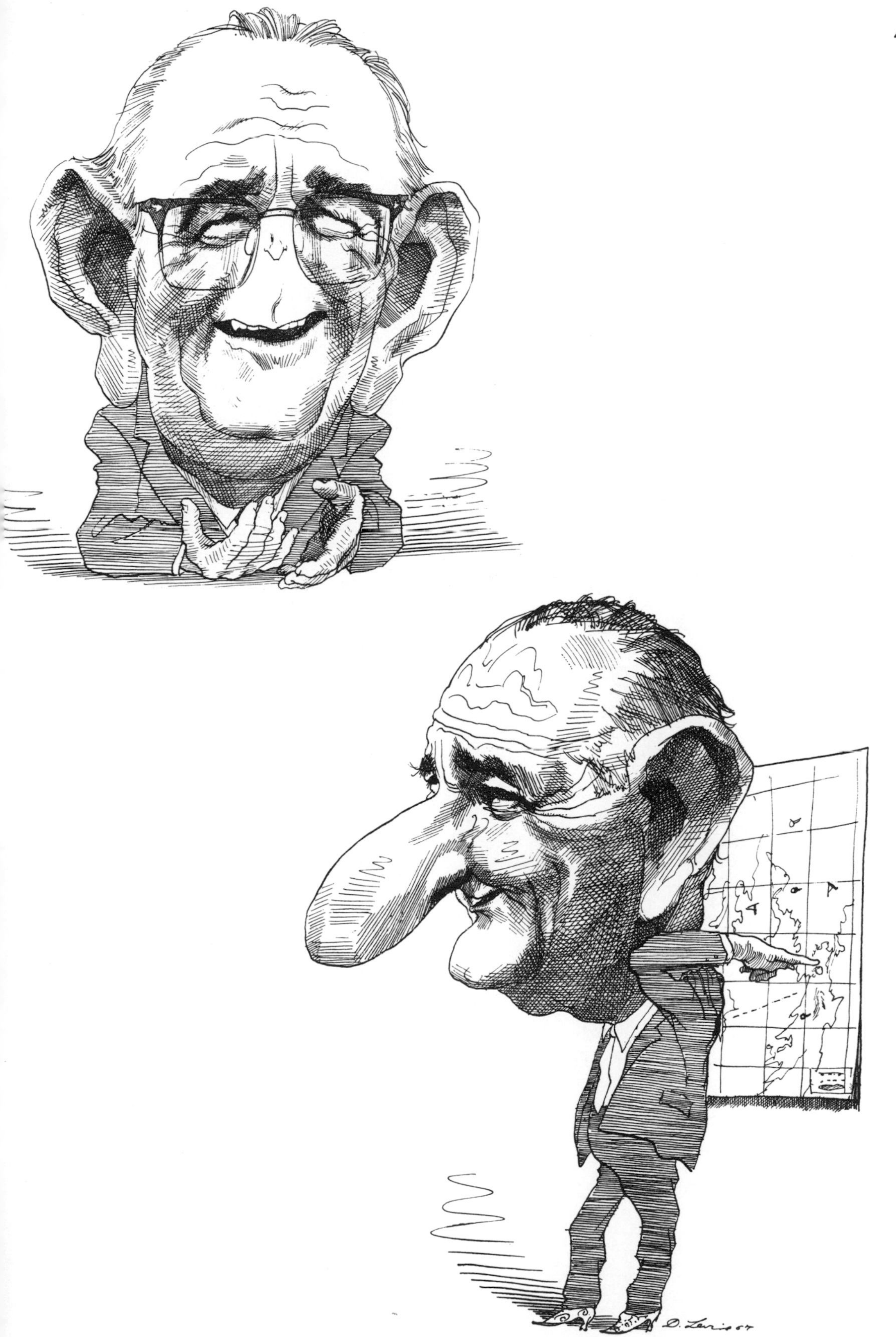

Let Me Tell You About My . . .

. . . Decoration.

Old Glory

Scars and Stripes

Allegories

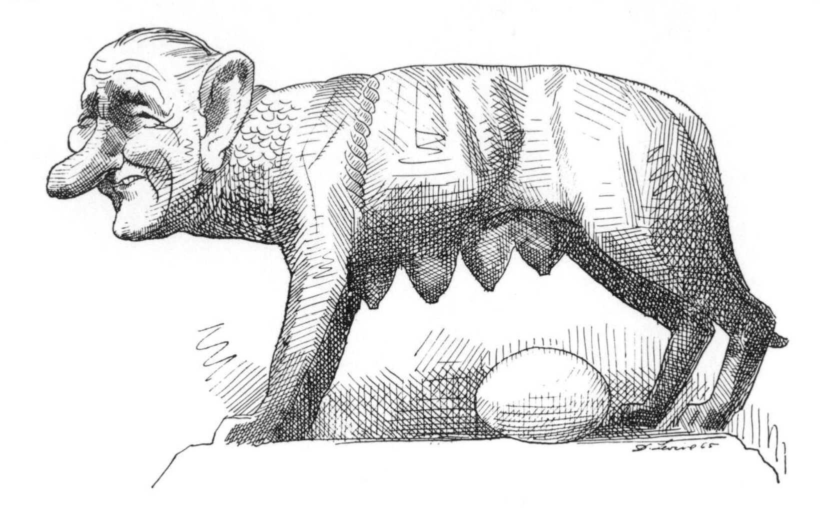

Friends, Enemies, and Bedfellows

Mme. Nhu

Brezhnev

Ky

Ho

Fulbright

The Team

III

See America First

Presidents Past

A Founding Father

WW and Couch

Available Man

HST and Artifacts

DDE

Diplomats and Cold Warriors

Acheson and Weapon

James Byrnes and Hat

Dean Rusk and Client

Kennan and Care

The Unsilenced Majority

Harriman on Limb

Fulbright on Favorite Path

Ball on Job

We Go Forward in Confidence

Hot Warriors

Blackjack

Georgie

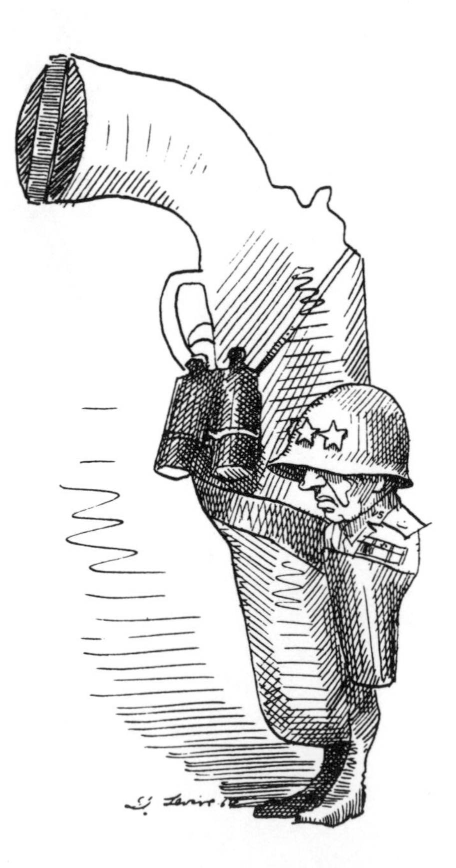

Doug

Marshall Plants

Maxwell Taylor Lands Softly

Curtis Lemay with Button

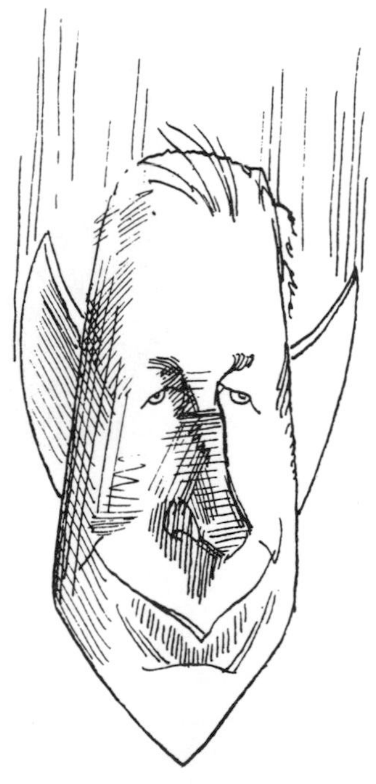

Thomas S. Power Arriving

Unidentified General

Warrior Rests

Law and Order

Chief Justice

Ramsey Clark

A Portfolio of Political Prophets, Scribes, and Scribblers

James Reston Balancing Good and Evil

I. F. Stone Uncovering Wickedness

Drew Pearson Viewing It

Harrison Salisbury and Weapon

Luce and Lucre

Spock with Impediment

Buckley with Audience

Theodore White (One Man Always Wins.)

FAMILY ALBUM

JPK

JFK and Friend

RFK

EMK and Neighbor

More Friends and Helpers

Mac

Walter Heller

Arthur Schlesinger

Schlesinger and Sorensen Deliver the Goods

YOUR LOCAL SPY AND COUNTERSPY

Dulles

F.B.I.

Joe McCarthy

Whittaker Chambers

Less Local

Fidel

Bay of Pigs

Along For The Ride

Reagan

Lindsay

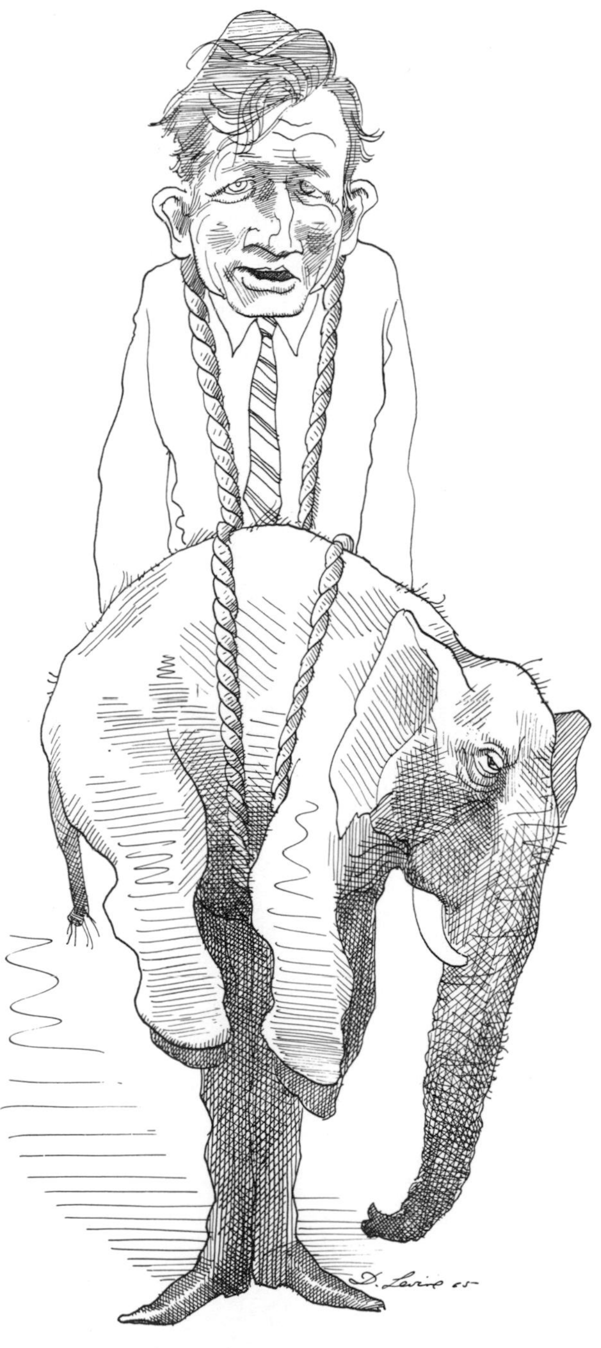

Gene

American Gallery

George Norris

Ev

Huey

Estes K.

Bayard

General Hershey

Adam

The Mayor

Romney

IV
World Tour

The British Then

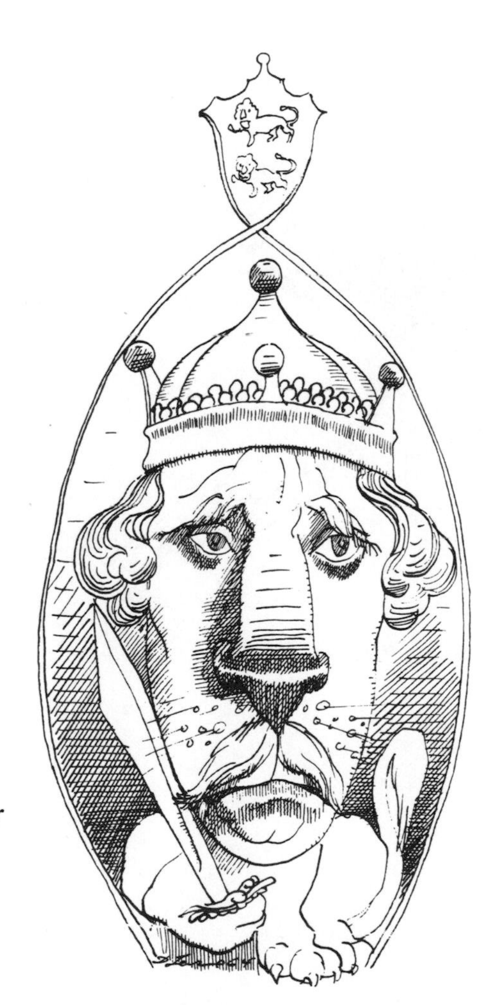

William the Conqueror

Henry VIII

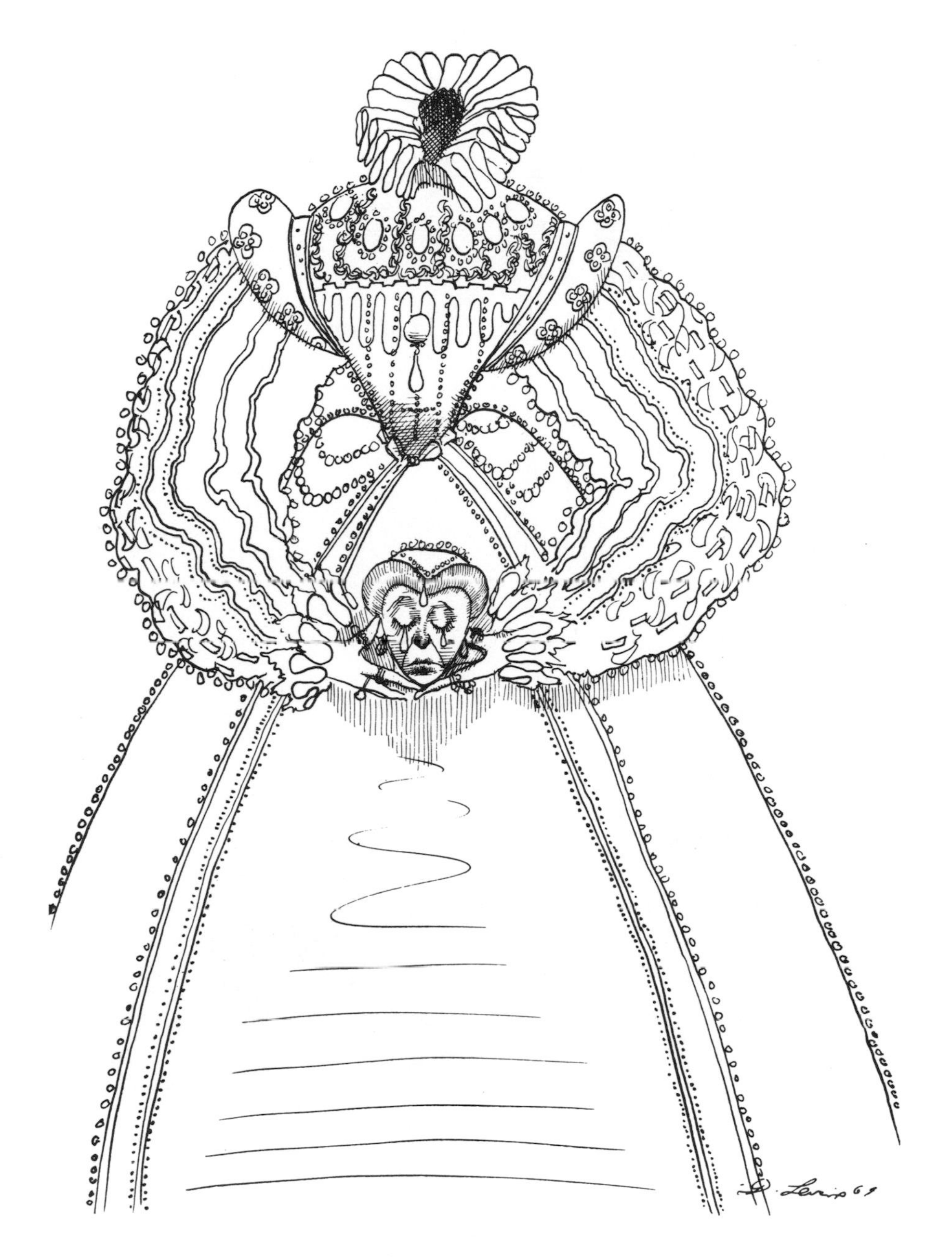

Mary, Queen of Scots

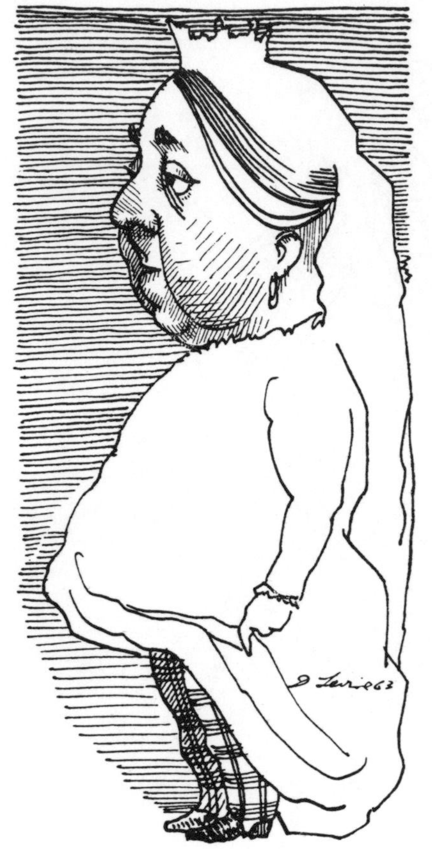

Mother

Son

Disraeli

Lloyd George

Asquith

Offenders of the Faith

The Offended

Empire

WSC

The British Since

Montgomery

Keynes

Eden

Macmillan with Friend

Richard Crossman

Chance Encounters

FDR, Joe, WSC

Nasser, Eden, and Hovering Presence

Eden and Dulles

Ludwig, Charles, and Harold

Family Reunion

Precursors, Successors, and General de Gaulle

Citizeness

Rousseau

Emperor

With Soldiers

Leon Blum

George Bidault

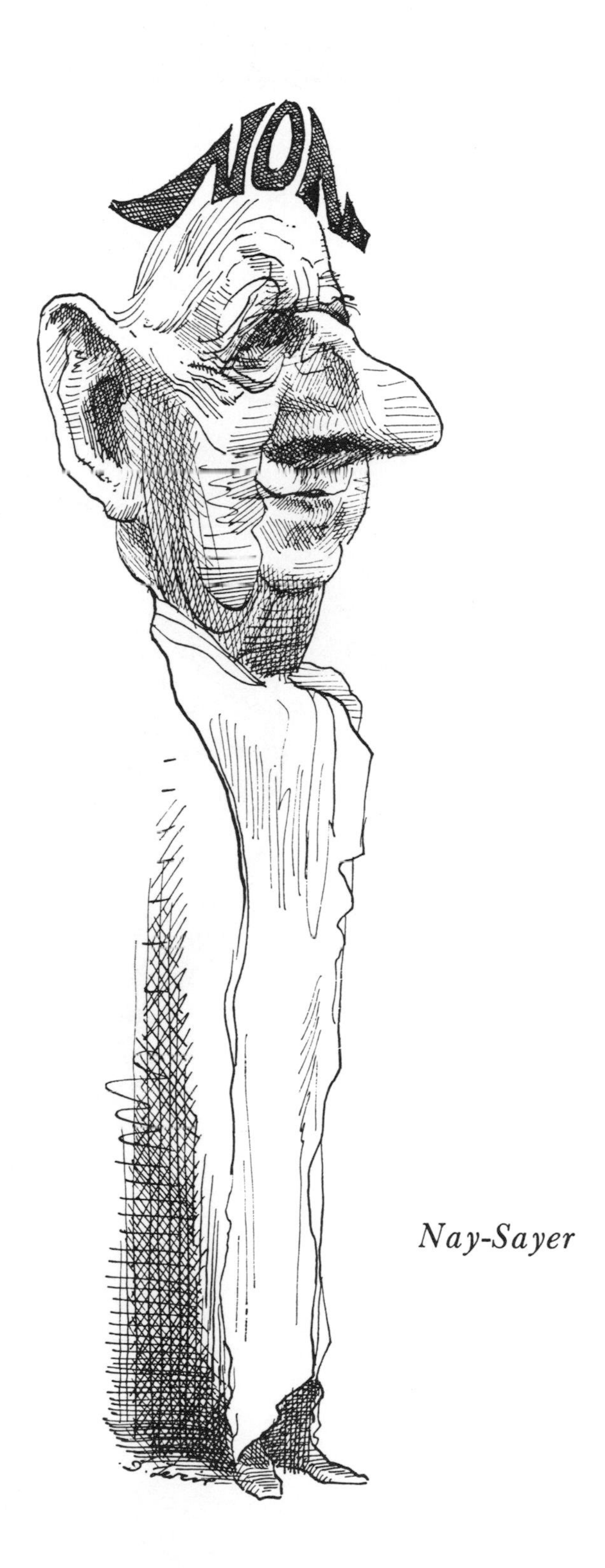

Nay-Sayer

de Gaulle

Pompidou

The Germans Pro and Con

Bismarck

Marx and Hegel

Marx and Pie

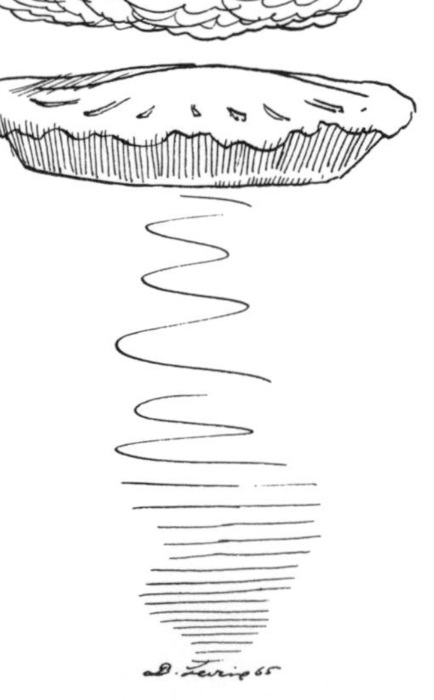

Rosa Luxemburg

Mouthpieces

Adenauer

Erhard

By Suez, East of Suez

Herzen

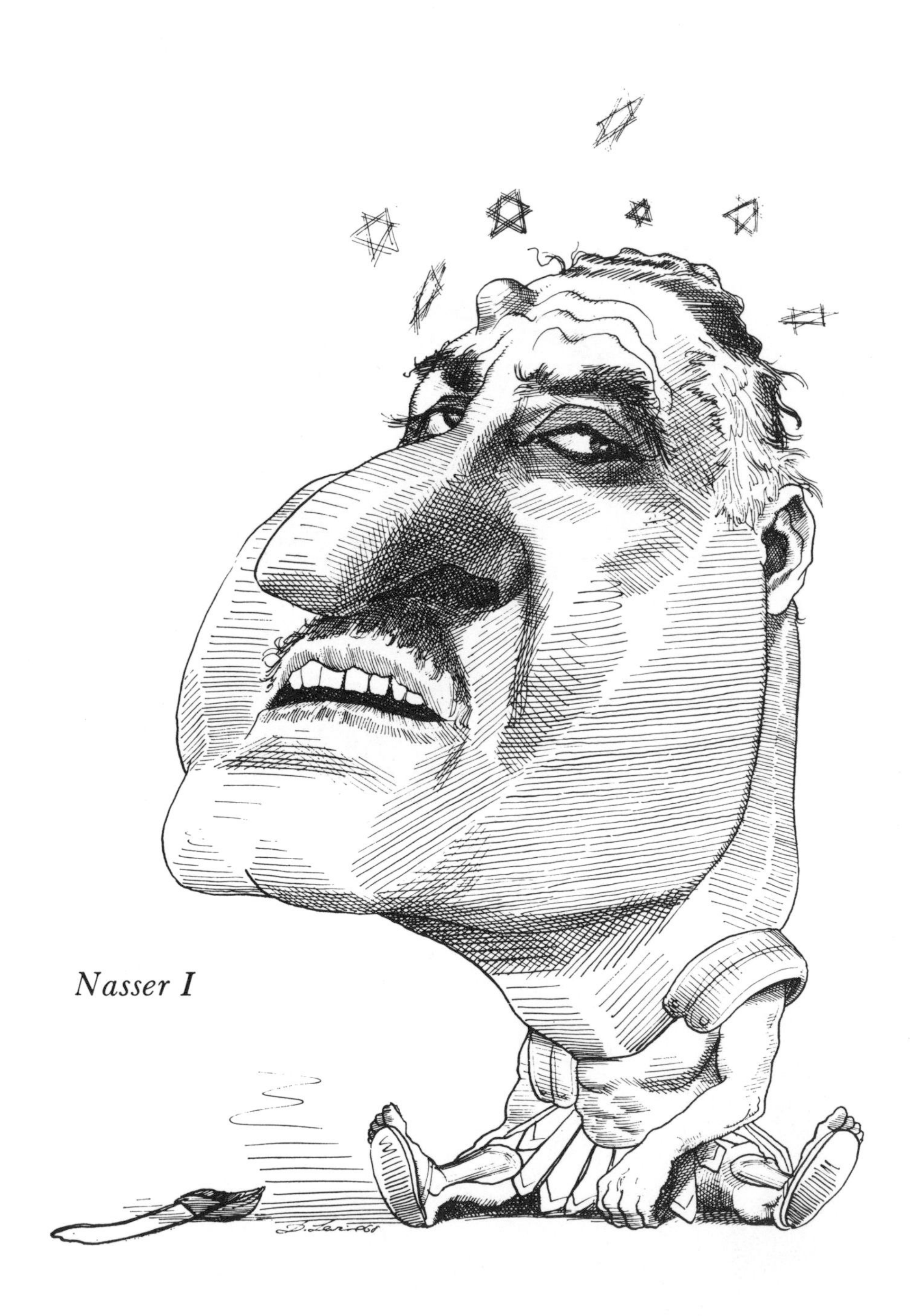

Nasser I

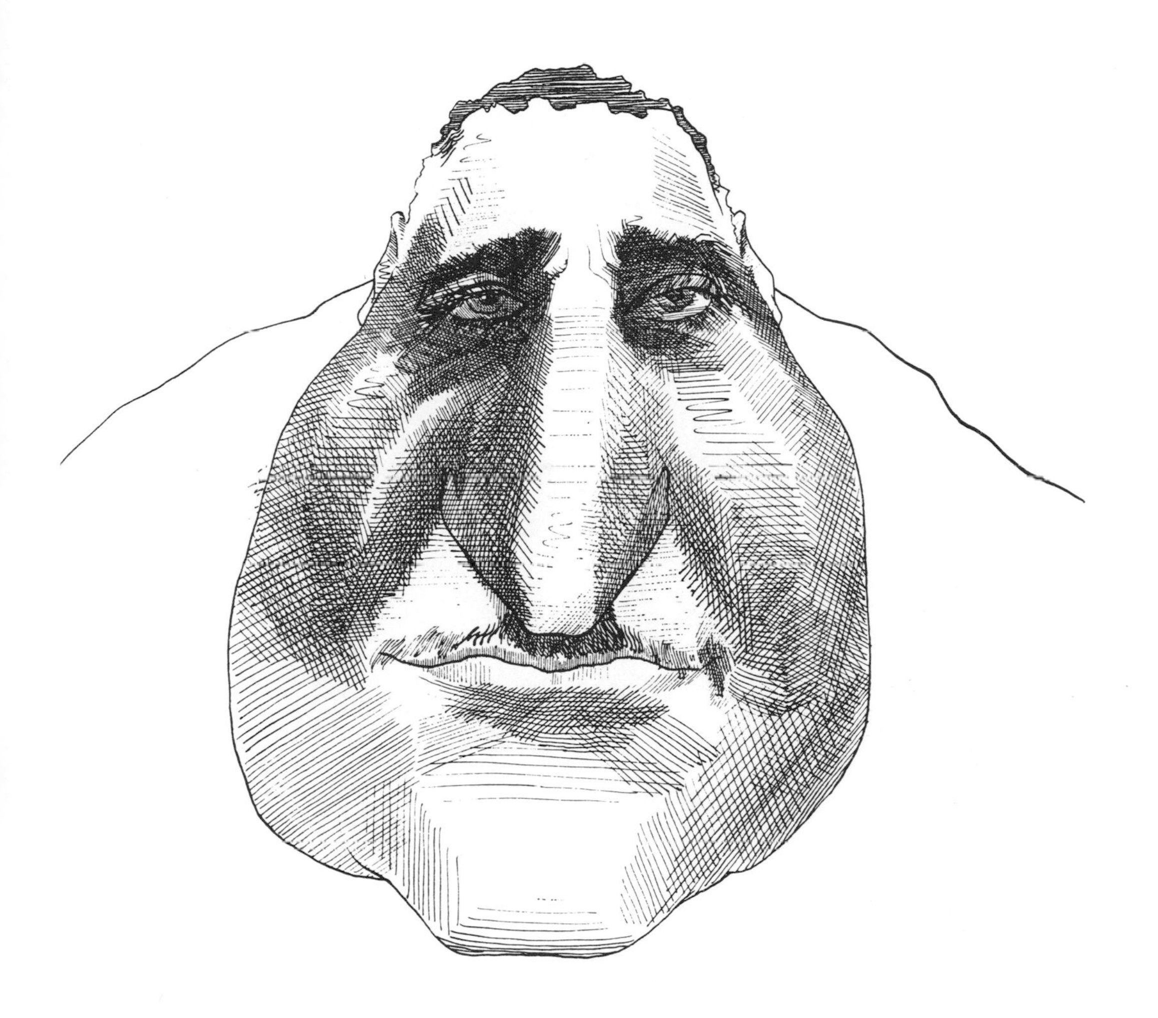

Nasser II

Multilateral Force

Added Starters, Also Rans

Austrian

Ethiopian

Italian I

Italian II: Togliatti

Greek

Spaniard

Nkrumah

Ben Gurion

Father and Child

Stalin and Silent Majority

Pallbearer

Svetlana and Friend

Svetlana Without Friend

The Other Russians

Lenin

Kerenski

Trotsky

Kosygin

Friends, Enemies, and Vice Versa

Marshall Ky and Mentor

Uncle Ho

Inscrutable Smiler

Warms Up

Cools off

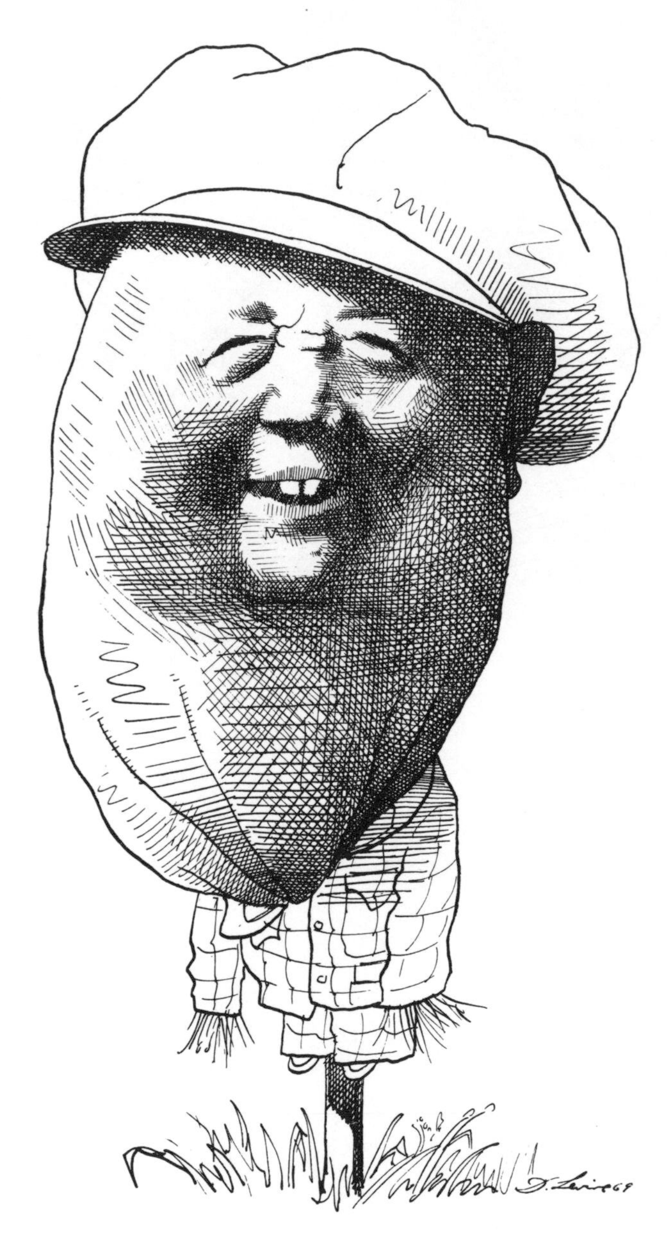

Scares Crows

V

World Dream and Nightmares

Saints, Prophets, Revolutionaries

Mahatma I

Mahatma II

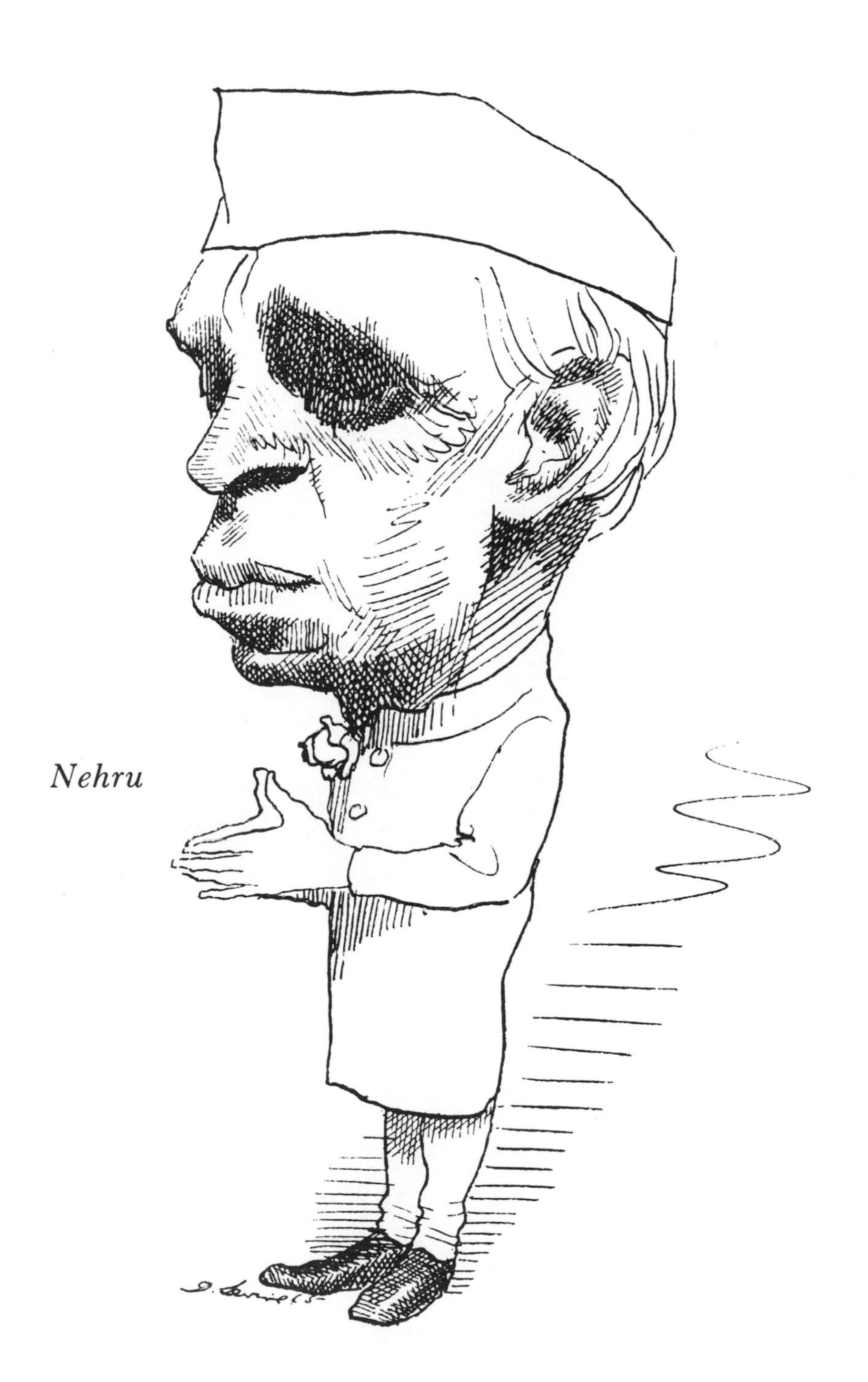

Nehru

Martin Luther King, Jr.

Paul Goodman

Herbert

LeRoi

Stokely

Elijah Muhammed

Dag Hammarskjöld

U Thant

U Thant and Goods

Papa Doc

Bernadette

Pillar of Society

INDEX